LADY GAGA

UNOFFICIAL

Publisher and Creative Director: Nick Wells
Project Editor: Polly Prior
Picture Research: Laura Bulbeck
Art Director: Mike Spender
Layout Design: Jane Ashley
Digital Design and Production: Chris Herbert

Special thanks to: Laura Bulbeck, Emma Chafer, Esme Chapman, Karen Fitzpatrick and
Dawn Laker

FLAME TREE PUBLISHING
Crabtree Hall, Crabtree Lane
Fulham, London SW6 6TY
United Kingdom
www.flametreepublishing.com

Website for this book: www.flametreepop.com

First published 2013

13 15 17 16 14
1 3 5 7 9 10 8 6 4 2

© 2013 Flame Tree Publishing Ltd

A CIP record for this book is available from the British Library upon request.

ISBN 978-0-85775-873-6

Printed in China

LADY GAGA

Hugh Fielder
Foreword by Malcolm Mackenzie

**FLAME TREE
PUBLISHING**

Contents

Foreword

For me there is no competition: Lady Gaga is the best pop star in the world. Not since the 1980s heyday of Michael Jackson, Madonna and Prince has a pop icon inspired global devotion like Stefani Germanotta. I was a fan from the moment I heard breezy debut single 'Just Dance' at the tail end of 2008. I went to see her very first club appearance at the Astoria in London, right before they tore it down. Despite brandishing her disco stick clumsily in roughly made iPod specs to a half empty auditorium, you could see she was a bit special. But when I first interviewed her I never dreamed she would become the mega-selling, taboo-busting, gender-swapping, generation-defining, record-breaking, smoldering fag-end, beef-fillet and Kermit-the-Frog-wearing artist she is today. Or that she would go on to produce three incredible albums in three short years.

Gaga has succeeded in changing the landscape of popular music. We can categorize music in the twenty-first century as BG and PG: Before-Gaga and Post-Gaga. It is no longer acceptable to turn up, sing a nice song and bob about from side to side on the stage as many artists did in the world BG. Gaga brought back drama and everyone looked drab in comparison. Suddenly her pop peers stepped up their game and became the best versions of themselves that they could.

But behind the image lies a unique voice and writing talent; Gaga is as comfortable singing jazz standards with Tony Bennett and knocking out piano ballads for Queen Elizabeth as she is spitting blood and making out with maligned religious figures. She is in a constant state of metamorphosis – some ideas work better than others – but we are always glad she made the effort. Put your paws up for Mother Monster.

Malcolm Mackenzie

Editor, We Love Pop

Why Gaga?

When you think of Lady Gaga, do you think of the meat dress or as her dressed as a man for the MTV Awards? Her androgynous, whacky yet sexy image is certainly part of her identity and is a means to represent her perception of her art. Don't be fooled though, this is one hard working lady, who has honed her talent from a young age.

Breaking Records

At the top of her game and the proud owner of five Grammy Awards, she has been voted the second Most Influential Woman of the decade by *Time* magazine, beating the Burmese political icon Aung San Suu Kyi, and is listed as the 45th Most Powerful Woman by *Forbes*, with earnings of $52 million as of May 2012.

And then there's the record sales: *The Fame* (2008) sold more than 17 million albums worldwide, and *Born This Way* (2011) shot straight to No. 1 in the US on release, with first-week sales of more than 1.1 million, the highest weekly total in seven years, and more than the next 42 albums in the chart combined. Within four months *Born This Way* sold five million copies worldwide.

It is not just Lady Gaga's albums that break records, however, she is the first artist to sell 20 million digital singles in America. 'Born This Way' was the fastest-selling single in the history of iTunes.

'Gaga's always been who I am.'

Lady Gaga

'I'm an outcast from the music industry. I don't have any friends in the business. I feel completely detached from the celebrity world. You never see me falling out of nightclubs.'

Lady Gaga

'The only big things I've purchased are
my dad's heart valve and a Rolls Royce
for their anniversary.'
Lady Gaga

Making Career Moves

Moving into an apartment in New York's bohemian Lower East Side in the summer of 2005, Stefani Germanotta set about forming a band. The Stefani Germanotta Band – also known as the SGBand – began rehearsing and recording a five-track demo, and started gigging early in 2006 at the nearby Bitter End Club, selling copies of their demo and an EP they recorded that spring called *Red And Blue*.

Stefani's first big break came when the band played a songwriters' showcase gig at the Cutting Room in June 2006 and were spotted by talent scout Wendy Starland. Impressed by her confidence, Wendy immediately contacted her boss, Rob Fusari, a multi-platinum record producer. Wendy said: 'I grabbed hold of her afterwards and said I was going to "change her life".'

Fusari and Starland set to work, improving Stefani's music and her image. Fusari persuaded her to drop the rock riffs and add dance beats to her songs. Together they co-wrote three songs that would eventually turn up on her first album: 'Paparazzi', 'Beautiful, Dirty, Rich' and 'Again Again'.

'I don't want to sound presumptuous but I've made it my goal to revolutionize pop music.'
Lady Gaga

Name Change

No one is sure when Stefani Germanotta changed her name to Lady Gaga. However, no one doubts that Queen's 1984 hit 'Radio Gaga' was the inspiration. The song was a favourite of Rob Fusari. 'Every day when Stef came into the studio, instead of saying hello I would start singing "Radio Gaga".' He says the name arose after a texting error: 'I typed Radio Gaga and it did an autocorrect so somehow "Radio" got changed to "Lady".' She texted back, 'That's it.' 'After that day she was Lady Gaga. She's like "Don't ever call me Stefani again".'

However, Wendy Starland says that the name came out of a brainstorming meeting before they started shopping around the record labels. And Lady Gaga herself said in an interview in 2009 that her 'realization of Gaga was five years ago, but Gaga's always been who I am'.

Movers And Shakers

The first record company to show an interest in Lady Gaga was Def Jam, the hip-hop and urban music label. She signed a contract in September 2006 with a reported advance of $850,000 and plans to release an album the following summer. However three months later the contract was terminated without explanation, but Lady Gaga was smart enough to waive part of her advance in exchange for ownership of the master tapes she had already produced – which contained two future hits. 'I went back to my apartment and I was so depressed. That's when I started the real devotion to my music and art,' she said.

'LA told me I was a star.'

Lady Gaga

Starlight Burlesque

Lady Gaga drowned her sorrows in the unfashionable glam-rock/art trash scene where she encountered performance artist Lady Starlight who introduced her to the joys of burlesque and go-go dancing. Together they formed Lady Gaga & The Starlight Revue with Gaga in little more than a bikini playing synthesizers and Starlight spinning beats as they danced to choreographed go-go moves beneath shiny disco balls and set alight jets of hairspray.

'Starlight and I bonded instantly over her love of heavy metal and my love of boys that listen to heavy metal.'

Lady Gaga

Gearing Up For The Fame

Lady Gaga was initially set up as a songwriter for The Pussycat Dolls and Britney Spears, while recording her own tracks with Moroccan/ Swedish producer RedOne. She recorded 'Just Dance', written with RedOne and Gaga's mentor, Akon, and the lights went on around Interscope records, and Gaga quickly found herself working with a choreographer on moves to match the music. It started to climb the US charts, just as *The Fame* album came out in August 2008, and finally made No. 1 in January 2009 – around the same time it topped the UK charts.

In contrast, the second single, the innuendo-laden 'Poker Face' (co-written with RedOne), took less than a month to hit the US top spot. Over the summer of 2009 the song went globally viral, eventually selling over 9 million copies. From this point on, Lady Gaga was impossible to ignore.

'Everyone was telling me I wasn't pop last year, and now look – so don't tell me what pop is. I know what pop is.'

Lady Gaga

*'I had this dream and I really wanted
to be a star. I was almost a monster
in the way that I was fearless with
my ambitions.'*

Lady Gaga

The Fame Monster

Originally planned as a bonus disc for a deluxe edition of *The Fame*, Lady Gaga decided to release the eight-track EP *The Fame Monster* as a standalone CD in November 2009. The first single, 'Bad Romance', was hailed as Lady Gaga's best yet and proof that she was more than a one-hit wonder, and peaked at No. 2 in the US. In the UK it topped the charts in December 2009, making Gaga the first lady to have three British No. 1 hits in a year.

The second single, 'Telephone', which is about preferring to dance rather than answer her boyfriend's call, was originally written for Britney Spears, but was rejected by her label. A third single, 'Alejandro', was a return to Europop territory with a Latin slant, keeping her on the airwaves for the second successive summer.

The Girl From New York City

Stefani Joanne Angelina Germanotta was born in Yonkers, a suburb of New York, on 28 March 1986. By the age of four she was singing along to the hits of Michael Jackson and Cyndi Lauper on a cheap plastic cassette player. When she was seven, her family moved to the Upper West Side of Manhattan. At the age of 11 she went to the private, all-girl Convent of the Sacred Heart on Manhattan's Upper East Side.

Early Life And Musical Talent

Her interest in music was roused after learning to pick out her favourite pop songs on her grandmother's piano at the age of five. She wrote her first song, a ballad, when she was 13 years old. The following year she began auditioning to appear at open-mic nights at various clubs. At high school she took leading roles in school musical productions, before moving on to study at the Tische School of Arts. After her first year she decided to take a break and focus on her musical career. Her father agreed to support her on the condition that she would resume her studies if things did not work out.

Well my music was different in high school. I was singing about love — you know, things I don't care about anymore.'

Lady Gaga

Under The Influence

As the biggest pop icon of the twenty-first century, comparisons with Madonna are inevitable; however, more unlikely influences include Britney Spears and Elton John. Indeed, Gaga grew up learning to play the piano Elton John's way – and you can still hear the impression that he has left. The two of them consummated their mutual admiration at the 2010 Grammies where they performed Elton's 'Your Song' and Gaga's 'Speechless'. They also recorded 'Hello Hello' for the Disney animation *Gnomeo & Juliet* (2011).

The greatest influence perhaps is Freddie Mercury; his fearless artistic extravagance and vocal style have been a constant inspiration for her. 'Freddie was unique – one of the biggest personalities in the whole of pop music,' she declares. 'He was not only a singer but a fantastic performer, a man of the theater and someone who constantly transformed himself. In short, a genius.'

'I guess you could say that I'm a bit of a fame Robin Hood. I want young people to know that they can be exactly who they want to be. There is an art to fame.'

Lady Gaga

Putting On The Style

From the start Lady Gaga has indulged her outrageous fashion sense. From her tea-party sunglasses to her Ice-Lady disco stick, Gaga has encouraged her fans to expect the unexpected. Many of her most eccentric outfits are known by their nicknames – the meat dress, the Kermit dress, the bubble dress, the red veil. To help realize her visions of fashion and style, Lady Gaga set up the Haus Of Gaga in 2008, a creative team to work on her costumes and stage designs.

Tour De Force

Lady Gaga got her first opportunity to put her concert show together when she landed the support slot on the reformed New Kids On The Block 27-date American tour in September 2008. She followed that tour early in 2009 with another support slot for The Pussycat Dolls on the European and Australian legs of their Doll Domination tour.

For her first headlining tour Lady Gaga was able to make use of the entire stage area and wasted no time in filling it up. The Fame Ball tour criss-crossed the US between March and May 2009 before Gaga headed off to Australia with The Pussycat Dolls. For the second leg, which toured around Europe from June to September, Gaga was finally able to use a live band consisting of musician friends from New York.

The first leg of the Monster Ball tour ran from November 2009 to January 2010, playing theatres in the US. The advance demand for tickets was so great that the tour was upgraded from theatres to arenas. The Monster Ball tour resumed in the UK in February 2010 and ran for the next 15 months, mainly around Europe and the US but also taking in Australia and finishing up in Mexico City 106 shows later.

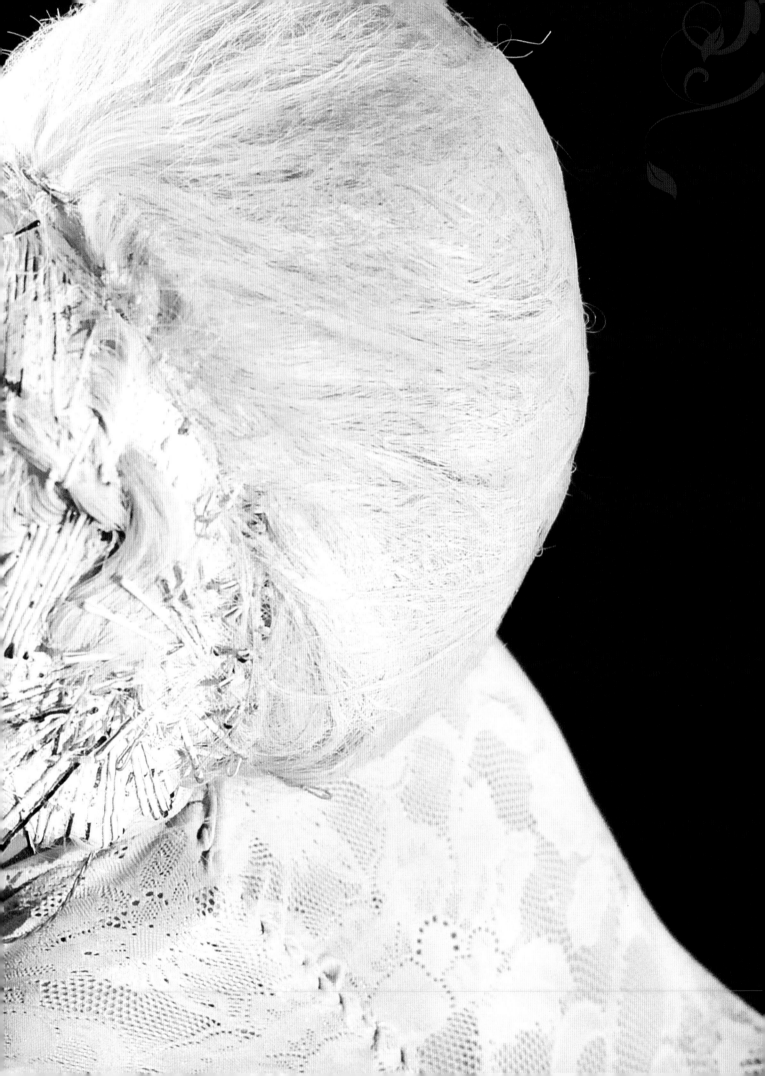

'I remember watching shows when I was little and dreaming about being on stage … I want to be that for somebody else.'

Lady Gaga

Born To Tour

Having set up a series of 'Haus parties' to promote the release of her *Born This Way* album, Lady Gaga revealed that her tour, the Born This Way Ball, would start in 2012, although she promised some one-off shows before then. Just as her Monster Ball Tour was extensive, the Born This Way Ball took in South America, India and Indonesia as well as the US, Europe and Australia – it was the highest grossing tour in 2012. Unfortunately, Gaga postponed shows in Chicago, Detriot and Hamilton due to illness, and on 13 February 2013 made an announcement that the remainder of the tour would be cancelled because of a hip injury that required surgery.

'It's the greatest post-apocalyptic house party that you've ever been to.'

Lady Gaga

Gaga's Little Monsters

The special relationship that Lady Gaga has built up with her fans has given her an intensely loyal following. From the beginning she encouraged her fans to follow her on Facebook and Twitter where she posted messages to them. She started referring to them as 'little monsters' – and to herself as 'mother monster' – before the release of *The Fame Monster* that included a Manifesto of Little Monsters in the Book of Gaga that came with the Super-Deluxe edition.

Giving It Back

Lady Gaga has used her influence to support her chosen causes and campaigns, including the 2010 Haitian earthquake and the 2011 Japanese earthquake and tsunami as well as homeless and children's charities in the US and UK.

Other causes reflect her personal beliefs. Having declared her bisexuality in 2009, she launched Viva Glam Gaga lipstick, with proceeds going to educating women on the risks of HIV and AIDS. She has campaigned for gay rights, appearing at the 2010 MTV Video Music Awards accompanied by four gay members of the American armed forces, and at Europride in Rome in 2011.

'Don't you ever let a soul in the world tell you that you can't be exactly who you are.'

Lady Gaga

'It's more annoying to me that people would insinuate that I don't like to be compared to Madonna.'

Lady Gaga

Born This Way

A remix album of Lady Gaga's biggest hits was inevitable, given the incredible success she had enjoyed with *The Fame* and *The Fame Monster*. *The Remix* (2010) was initially released in Japan in March 2010, selling more than 250,000 copies. A revised edition of the album came out in the rest of the world during the summer of 2010 and sales have passed half a million, making it one of the top ten bestselling remix albums.

She's a great musician, she's a great singer, and she's laughing when she's doing it, the same way that I am.'

Marilyn Manson

Broadening Horizons

Lady Gaga started working on her second 'proper' album, *Born This Way*, in the spring of 2010 and recorded the songs at various studios around the world during her relentless touring schedule. She was not just broadening out geographically but musically. Gaga's influences now included new wave, mainstream rock and opera, and the synthesizers sometimes gave way to electric guitars and violins. Guest appearances on the album included Queen guitarist Brian May and saxophonist Clarence Clemons from Bruce Springsteen's East Street Band (who died less than a month after the album was released in May 2011).

Born Controversial

The first two singles from the *Born This Way* album sparked condemnation from religious groups and even some governments. Lady Gaga's strong stance on sexuality and feminism on the album's title song was deemed 'immoral' by fundamentalist Christian and Islamic organizations, while the references to Mary Magdalene in the second single, 'Judas', provoked anger from the Catholic Church. Radio stations in Malaysia were ordered to edit the lyrics of 'Born This Way' by the government. And 'Judas' was banned in Lebanon after protests from the Catholic Information Centre – the government even temporarily banned *Born This Way*.

Digital Domination

No one has taken more advantage of the digital era than Lady Gaga, who has become the first artist to sell more than 20 million single downloads. Gaga's digital album sales highlight the rapid growth of the market. US digital sales of *The Fame* have topped a million, while *Born This Way* had digital sales of more than 600,000 in its first week. Amazon accounted for some 440,000 sales with a two-day promotional campaign offering the album for 99 cents, a marketing ploy that cost the company over $3 million.

'I'm just trying to change the world,

one sequin at a time.'

Lady Gaga

'Don't be a drag, just be a queen.'

Lyrics from 'Born This Way'

A Social Whirl

Lady Gaga has voraciously used social networking and free-stream sites to promote her career – she even has her own social networking site Little Monsters. She tops the Social 50, a chart that measures how popular people are on social media sites, including Facebook, Twitter and YouTube. In July 2010 Gaga became the first living person to have 10 million followers on Facebook.

Gaga is smart about using free-streaming sites like YouTube, too and uses her channel not just for her official music videos but also to keep her followers closely engaged, such as the clip from a Toronto concert when she invited 10-year-old Maria Aragon, whose cover of 'Born This Way' had recently gone viral on YouTube, to join her on stage. They sang the song in front of 20,000 people and Gaga's eyes welled with tears as Maria gave a shoutout to her family and friends in Winnipeg, Canada.

'Ten million monsters! I'm speechless,

we did it. It's an illness how I love you.'

Lady Gaga

The Lady Gaga Effect

Lady Gaga is not just a digital queen, she reigns supreme over the traditional media scene too. She has appeared on over 100 magazine covers and all of them experienced a circulation surge as a result. This was particularly true in 2010, the year of Gaga-mania in the media. *Rolling Stone* and *Cosmopolitan* both scored their biggest-selling issues of the year with their Gaga covers. Only Angelina Jolie was able to pull in more readers at *Vanity Fair*.

The covers were invariably flamboyant but not risqué, except for the British *Q* magazine, which was banned in the US for displaying the lower portion of one breast – an infringement of New York State law. How the moral guardians missed the strap-on dildo beneath Gaga's trousers remains a mystery.

'Don't you think that what's on the cover of a magazine is quite artificial?'

Lady Gaga

The 3D Screen

The Super-Deluxe edition of *The Fame Monster* released in December 2009 included a pair of 3D glasses 'for things that will happen soon'. In March 2010 Lady Gaga tweeted that 'the Monster Ball DVD is going to be released and it will be in 3D!' However, there was no further news until February 2011 when Gaga told TV chat-show host Jay Leno she was filming her New York Madison Square Garden concerts that month for an HBO television special that aired in May – but not in 3D. More news on the DVD is awaited.

Meanwhile, Gaga's 3D activities have been restricted to her fingernails – picking up on the 3D nail fashion that started in Japan with girls decorating their extended nails with gels, glitter, figurines and flowers. Gaga has been seen with jewellery and tiny boxes on her nails, which are true works of art. One of the Japanese-designed, intricate black and gold acrylic nails that she wore during her Born This Way Ball was sold at auction to an unnamed Gaga fan in June 2013 for a staggering US$12,000.

'Some artists want your money so they can buy Range Rovers and diamond bracelets, but I don't care about that kind of stuff. I want your soul.'

Lady Gaga

'I am focused on the work.
I am constantly creating. I live and
breathe my work. I love my work.
There's no stopping. I didn't create
the fame, the fame created me.'

Lady Gaga

The Silver Screen

For years the media have been speculating about Lady Gaga's movie plans. In August 2010 (traditionally a slow month for real news), UK tabloid *News Of The World* reported that Gaga was in discussions to make a 'block-buster' movie, pitched somewhere between Michael Jackson's *Moonwalker* (1988) and Beyoncé's role in *Dreamgirls* (2006). There was even a director lined up, Bryan Singer, who directed *The Usual Suspects* (1995) and *X-Men* (2000). Gaga's office denied the story.

Exactly a year later, more stories claimed that Gaga was in 'secret discussions' to play Amy Winehouse in a biopic of the late singer's life. Although Gaga has expressed her admiration for Winehouse, the rest appears to be Hollywood gossip. Gaga did express, however, if making a biopic of her life, she would like Marisa Tomei to play her part.

For fans, dreams of seeing Gaga on the big screen is about to become a reality. Alongside an all-star cast, including Danny Trejo, Mel Gibson, Jessica Alba and Charlie Sheen (credited as Carlos Estevez), Gaga makes her first film appearance in action flick *Machete Kills*, written and directed by Robert Rodriguez, which is due to be released in September 2013 in the US.

'I'm working on bringing the instant film camera back as part of the future.'

Lady Gaga

'For me, more than anything, I want to do something important. It's gotta be important. If it's coming out of my mouth, if it's going on my body, if it's going on TV, it better be important.'

Lady Gaga

The Future Is Gaga

Despite undergoing hip surgery, you can be sure that Lady Gaga is not resting on her laurels. Though confined to a wheelchair for some time, the Lady has been busy working on two albums, one a collaboration with jazz legend Tony Bennett and her long-awaited fourth studio album *ARTPOP*, with a release date of November 2013, which is both album and app, allowing fans to access an 'interactive worldwide community.'

Bennett, who previously worked with Gaga on the song 'The Lady Is A Tramp' for his album *Bennett II*, can't praise her highly enough, saying 'She's phenomenal. I get along great with her. She's looking forward to it and so am I.'

Lady Gaga Vital Info

Birth Name	Stefani Joanne Angelina Germanotta
Birth Date	28 March 1986
Birth Place	New York City
Height	1.53 m (5 ft 1 in)
Nationality	American
Hair Colour	Brown; usually dyed platinum blonde
Eye Colour	Hazel
Alter Egos	Lady Gaga, Jo Calderone

Online

ladygaga.com:	Official site with info on Haus of Gaga, news, events and lyrics
ladygaga.co.uk:	Official UK site with a forum, gallery, shop and more
myspace.com/ladygaga:	Check this site out for the Lady's latest songs, videos and tour updates
ladygaganow.net:	Packed with resources for fans, such as interviews, videos, pictures and downloads
facebook.com/ladygaga:	Check out Lady Gaga's latest writing on the wall
twitter.com/ladygaga:	Join the millions of other followers at @ladygaga
flametreepop.com:	Celebrity, fashion and pop news, with loads of links, downloads and free stuff!

Acknowledgements

Hugh Fielder (Author)

Hugh Fielder has been writing about rock music for 35 years. He has witnessed and interviewed the great and the good, the not-so-good and the frankly useless. His main qualification for writing about Lady Gaga is that he took his daughters to see Madonna in her 80s heyday - twice. He is at a loss to explain why they later became such big fans of Wilson Phillips.

Malcolm Mackenzie (Foreword)

Malcolm Mackenzie is the editor of *We Love Pop*. He started as a professional pop fan writing for teen titles like *Top of the Pops*, *Bliss* and *TV Hits* before moving into the adult market working for *GQ*, *Glamour*, *Grazia*, *Attitude*, and newspapers such as *The Times*, *The Sunday Times*, *The Guardian* and *thelondonpaper* where he was Music Editor for three years before returning to the teen sector to launch *We Love Pop*.

Picture Credits

All images © **Getty Images**: FilmMagic: front cover & 21, 47; Getty Images Entertainment: 1, 3, 7 & back cover, 8, 15, 18, 24, 32, 38, 42, 44; WireImage: 11, 12, 16, 23, 26, 28, 31, 35, 41.